monday
morning®

ENERGY AND MACHINES

By Lynn Cohen

Illustrated by Philip Chalk

Publisher: Roberta Suid
Editor: Mary McClellan
Design and production: Susan Pinkerton

monday morning®

Monday Morning is a registered trademark of
Monday Morning Books, Inc.

Entire contents copyright ©1988 by Monday Morning
Books, Inc., Box 1680, Palo Alto, California 94302

ISBN 0-912107-78-2

Printed in the United States of America
9 8 7 6 5 4 3 2 1

CONTENTS

Chapter One: Energy Experiments   7
    Mechanical Energy
    Magnetic Energy
    Radiant Energy
    Electrical Energy

Chapter Two: Science & the Curriculum   29
    Language Arts
    Math
    Social Living

Chapter Three: Science & the Creative Arts   45
    Art
    Creative Movement
    Literature

INTRODUCTION

How do we use energy? How do machines makes things easier for us? How does a flashlight work? *Energy and Machines* offers children four to seven years old the opportunity to explore basic science principles through hands-on experiments and to apply what they learn to the world around them.

Classroom-tested projects encourage children to exercise their sense of wonder as well as their beginning problem-solving and creative thinking abilities. The activities in *Energy and Machines* guide children to be good observers and to make conclusions based on their observations. Children also develop important thinking skills such as categorizing, comparing, and cause and effect. The activities in the book do not focus exclusively on science. They also integrate the experiments with math, language arts, social living, art, and creative movement activities.

Most of these ideas have been field tested with early childhood students in the East Williston School District in New York, in a nursery school called Kids Korner in Huntington, Long Island, and with the author's own young children, Vicky and Mark. The activities have also been tested in numerous in-service workshops for preschool and primary teachers, who felt these activities were useful and appropriate for this age group.

All children, however, are not the same. They have diversified interests, abilities, and emotions. It is important to consider individual differences when using this book. For the classroom teacher, whole class or small group instruction is recommended. Many activities provide for individual differences in the section "Variations."

Background Information

Energy is what helps us do work. Mechanical energy is used to set an object in motion, such as winding up a clock or pushing or pulling an object. Electrical energy is used to turn on a lamp or operate a record player. Magnetic energy is invisible but it is generated by the motion of electrons or electric currents. Electric motors operate based upon the basic law of magnetism: like poles of a magnet repel and unlike poles attract each other. Radiant energy travels through air and is used to heat our homes.

Format of the Book

Energy and Machines is divided into four chapters. Chapter one is designed to help children think logically and productively, especially about real, concrete things. The experiments have the following format:

Problem: The title poses a question that asks students to think, discuss, and hypothesize answers. Children may make predictions about ways to solve the problem.

Materials: A general list of supplies is provided for each activity. Adjust the quantities according to the number of children involved.

Preparation: This section lists steps taken by the adult before beginning the activity. Most activities call for active involvement on the part of the children. However, when an experiment is an adult demonstration because of safety considerations, this is indicated in the preparation section.

Activity: This section lists the steps in the activity. Children are encouraged to explore and discover.

Observations: Children are encouraged to sharpen their awareness of what they see or experience in the activity.

Variation: Variations are listed for certain experiments, often suggesting adaptations of the experiments for children who are able to read and write or do math computations.

Things to Wonder About: These questions and follow-up activities are designed to help children question the world around them and to extend what they've learned to their daily life.

In chapters two and three, "Science and the Curriculum" and "Science and the Creative Arts," energy and machines is the organizing theme for language arts, math, social living, art, literature and movement. The focus in chapter two is on higher level thinking skills and creativity. Self-esteem is fostered through discussion, problem solving, and open-ended activities.

In chapter three, art activities emphasize the process, not the final product. The art activities are open-ended and will not be threatening to children who don't know how to draw. The creative movement activities encourage children to express themselves in a variety of creative ways. Chapters two and three have the following format:

Materials: A list of supplies is provided for each activity. Adjust according to the number of children doing the activity.

Preparation: This sections lists anything the adult needs to do before beginning the activity.

Activity: This lists the steps in the activity.

Variations: Variations are listed for certain activities, often suggesting adaptations for children who are able to read and write or do math computations.

The literature section is a resource list of related children's books for parents and teachers to read to children. Teachers should read children these selections during their story hour. Selections can be left in the classroom library or by the science center for children to look at or read.

Chapter One:

Energy Experiments

MECHANICAL ENERGY

How can you make a ball roll uphill?

Materials: Plank, block or books, small ball

Preparation: Set up an inclined plane by resting one end of the plank on the block or a pile of books.

Activity: Ask the children to think of different ways to make a ball roll up the inclined plane. Place the ball at the bottom of the plank, and have the children take turns giving the ball a push.

Observations: What happens when you give the ball a push? What happens if you give the ball a harder push?

Variation: Set up two inclined planes opposite each other. Have the children predict what will happen if you roll a ball down one inclined plane. Demonstrate how a ball can roll down one inclined plane and roll up another if given a hard push.

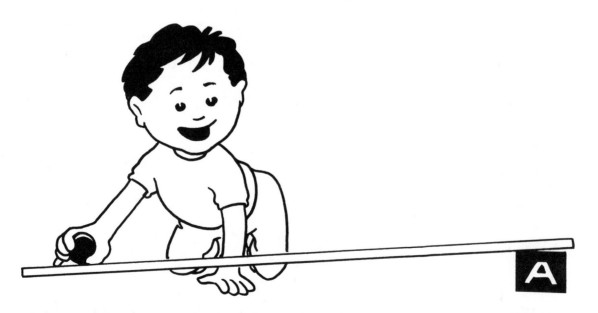

Which objects roll the farthest?

Materials: Plank, block or books, top, ball, spring, spool, can, rectangular and cylindrical blocks of wood, round pencil, hexagonal pencil, masking tape

Preparation: Set up an inclined plane, using the plank and the block or books.

Activity: Show the children the different objects and have them sort them into groups. Then have the children predict which objects will roll the farthest. Let each object roll down the plank. Mark how far each object rolls with masking tape.

Observations: Which objects rolled the farthest? How are they alike? Which objects rolled in a straight line?

Variation: Older children can measure the distances each object rolled by using rulers, yardsticks, or measuring tape.

Things to Wonder About: Why are balls round? Would a square ball roll?

Can you balance blocks on a seesaw?

Materials: Plank, cylindrical block, two triangular blocks, blocks of various sizes

Preparation: Discuss levers and how they are used to lift things. Make a seesaw (a lever) with the plank and blocks: Balance the plank on the cylindrical block. Use the two triangular blocks as wedges to hold the cylindrical block in place. This is an activity that needs careful supervision.

Activity: Collect blocks of different sizes and weights. Have the children experiment with putting different blocks on the seesaw. Have them try balancing blocks of equal size, heavy blocks and light blocks, and a different number of blocks on each side. Help the children discover that moving things closer to or farther from the center (the fulcrum) can help them balance some things.

Observations: Which side is heavier? Which side is lighter? How many little blocks does it take to balance a big block?

Things to Wonder About: How could you balance a heavy block with a light block? How would you make your side of a seesaw go down if someone bigger were sitting on the other end?

Can a lever help lift something?

Materials: Books, string, ruler, chalkboard eraser

Preparation: Tie the books together with a string.

Activity: Have the children pick up the books by the string using one finger. Then put the books on a table, and put one end of the ruler underneath the books. Rest the eraser under the ruler. Have the children try lifting the books, using the ruler as a lever.

Observations: Is it easier to lift the books by hand or with a lever? Move the position of the eraser closer to you. What happens?

Things to Wonder About: Can you balance a friend on a seesaw by moving farther from or closer to the center?

Can wheels help move something heavy?

Materials: Heavy box, wagon

Activity: Have the children try to move a heavy box by sliding and pushing it. Ask if they can think of other ways to move the box. Put the box in the wagon, and have the children pull the wagon.

Observations: Which way of moving the box was easier?

Variation: Have children examine a toy truck. Show the wheels. What holds the wheels on the left and right sides together? Explain that we usually find two wheels on either end of a long rod called an axle. Give children empty spools of thread and a nail and ask them to make a wheel and axle.

Things to Wonder About: What toys in the classroom move on wheels? How would the objects move if they didn't have wheels? What other things do we use that have wheels? Why don't boats have wheels?

On which surface will the car travel the farthest?

Materials: Toy car, yarn

Activity: Have the children examine the toy car. Ask them to predict whether the car would roll the farthest on a bare surface, on a rug, or on cement. Have the children roll the car on the different surfaces. Use the yarn to measure the distances the car traveled.

Observations: On which surface did the car travel the farthest?

Variation: Older children can use rulers and yardsticks to measure the distances.

Things to Wonder About: How are the surfaces different? What types of roads are hard to drive on? Can you roller-skate on dirt? On which surface is it easier to roller-skate?

How do springs help with work?

Materials: Slinky toy, discarded clock

Activity: Have two children pull a Slinky, and then have one of them let go. Have the children push a Slinky closed between their hands. Then have them pull their hands apart. Have a child find the spring in a clock.

Observations: What happens to the Slinky when you let go? What does the Slinky look like when you pull it apart? What does it look like when you push it together? Children will discover that a spring will always go back to its original shape after it was pushed or pulled.

Things to Wonder About: What types of toys have springs? How do the springs make toys or clocks work? What do springs do in a bed or in a couch cushion?

MAGNETIC ENERGY

Which objects stick to magnets?

Materials: Magnet, two bags of small objects

Preparation: Fill two lunch bags with a variety of junk objects.

Activity: Take the objects out of one bag. Have the children touch the magnet to each object. Put the objects that stuck to the magnet in one group. Ask the children to tell you how the objects in that group are alike. Then take the objects out of the second bag. Ask the children to predict which objects will stick to the magnet. Then have them test their predictions.

Observations: Which objects stuck to the magnet? How are those objects alike? Were your predictions correct?

Things to Wonder About: What other things might stick to a magnet? Where have you seen magnets used?

Can you feel a magnet's force?

Materials: Magnet, nail

Activity: Have the children hold a magnet near their hand. Then have them move the magnet close to their lips and then cheeks. Then have them hold the magnet in one hand and the nail in the other. Have them slowly move the magnet and nail closer to each other until they are touching. Then have the children pull the nail and magnet apart.

Observations: What happens when you bring the magnet close to the nail? What do you feel? What do you feel when you try to pull the nail away from the magnet?

Things to Wonder About: Why do you think you can't feel the magnet's force when you hold it next to your skin? What happens when you hold the like poles of two magnets together? The unlike poles?

Which is the strongest part of a magnet?

Materials: Bar magnet, horseshoe magnet, shallow box with clear plastic cover, iron filings, paper clips

Activity: Ask the children to predict which areas have the greatest magnetic force on a horseshoe magnet and on a bar magnet: the middle or the ends. Have the children test their predictions using paper clips. Then have the children hold a bar magnet under the box with plastic cover. Pour iron filings into the box and have the children watch what happens as they move the magnet. Repeat the experiment using the horseshoe magnet.

Observations: What do you see? What kind of pattern or design do the filings create? Where do you see the most iron filings? Which is the strongest part of a magnet? Which is the weakest part?

Things to Wonder About: What other shapes of magnets have you seen?

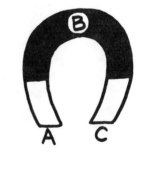

Will a magnet's force go through glass and water?

Materials: Paper clips, glass, clear bowl, water, magnet

Preparation: Place paper clips inside the glass. Fill the bowl with water. Put paper clips inside the bowl.

Activity: Have the children place the magnet on the outside of the glass, as close to the paper clips as possible. Have them move the magnet up and down the glass and observe the paper clips. Then have them try to get the paper clips out of the bowl of water by putting the magnet in the bowl.

Observation: Does a magnet's force go through glass? Does a magnet's force go through water?

Variation: Will a magnet's force go through a thick object? Put paper clips on top of a book. Hold the magnet under the bottom of the book. Can you move the paper clips with the magnet? Try putting the paper clips on the inside of the back cover and the magnet underneath the cover. Can you move the paper clips?

Things to Wonder About: What other objects will a magnet's force pass through?

How can you make a temporary magnet?

Materials: Magnet, nail, paper clips

Activity: Have the children hold the magnet in one hand and the nail in the other. Have them rub the nail in one direction (upward or downward) on the magnet. After they have rubbed for two minutes, ask them to try to pick up the paper clips using the nail.

Observations: Will the nail magnet pick up the other objects?

Things to Wonder About: What will happen if you drop your nail magnet on the floor a few times? Will the nail act as a magnet tomorrow? Which magnetic force is permanent, the horseshoe magnet's or the nail magnet's?

RADIANT ENERGY

How do things feel after they're left in the sun?

Materials: Two pie pans, sand, two coins, two black plastic bags

Activity: Fill the pie pans with sand. Put one pan of sand, one coin, and one garbage bag in the direct sunlight. Put the other pan, coin, and bag in the shade. After a while, have the children feel and compare the difference between the objects. Let the children's sense of touch act as a thermometer. Blindfold the children, and let them touch the objects.

Observations: Which objects feel warmer? Try feeling them with your hands and feet.

Things to Wonder About: How does the inside of a car feel on a hot day? What else feels warm when left in the sun?

Can the sun produce heat?

Materials: Magnifying glass, sheet of paper

Preparation: This is an adult demonstration. Caution children to avoid playing with the magnifying glass or placing a hand between the paper and the magnifying glass.

Activity: On a sunny day, hold the magnifying glass over a piece of paper outside in the sunlight. Move the magnifying glass up and down above the piece of paper until the light comes to a point. Hold it there a few seconds. Note: Do NOT have the children stare at or touch the point of light.

Observations: What happened to the paper? What made the hole in the paper? What does this tell you about what the sun does for us?

Things to Wonder About: Why do you feel warm in sunlight but cold in the shade? What is the sun made of that gives so much heat? Why don't astronauts explore the sun?

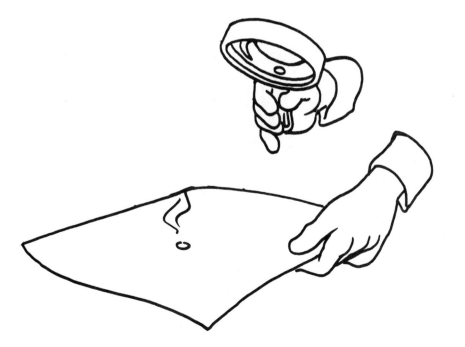

How can you put out a candle's flame?

Materials: Safety matches, votive candle, pie tin, glass jar, water, sand, baking soda

Preparation: This is an adult demonstration. Discuss safety precautions when using matches. Make sure that the children understand that matches should be lit only by adults or with adult supervision. Have a fire extinguisher handy when doing experiments involving fire.

Activity: Place the candle on the pie tin, and light the candle. Place a glass jar over the burning candle. What happens? Repeat using sand, baking soda, and water. Explain to the children that the lack of air (oxygen) makes the fire go out.

Observations: What happens when the jar is put over the candle? What happens when sand, baking soda, or water is used?

Things to Wonder About: What other things can you use to put out a fire?

What happens when objects are rubbed together?

Materials: wooden board, sheet of sandpaper

Preparation: Have the children rub their hands together very quickly for a minute and ask them what their hands feel like. Explain that this rubbing action is called friction and produces heat.

Activity: Have the children feel the board and the sandpaper. Have them sand the board very quickly and then touch the sanded board and sandpaper.

Observations: Do the board and sandpaper feel warm after it's sanded? Compare the way the board felt before and after it was rubbed.

ELECTRICAL ENERGY

How can you make static electricity?

Materials: Puffed wheat, balloon, wool

Preparation: Blow up a balloon. Crumble a few kernels of puffed wheat. This experiment should be performed on a day with low humidity.

Activity: Have the children try to pick up the puffed wheat with the balloon. Then have them rub the balloon on a piece of wool and try to pick up the puffed wheat with the balloon.

Observations: What happened the first time you tried to pick up the puffed wheat? What happened after you rubbed the balloon and tried?

Variation: What happens if the balloon is wet?

Things to Wonder About: Have you seen static electricity when you combed your hair? In what other ways have you experienced static electricity?

How can you make a newspaper stay on the wall?

Materials: Newspaper or sheet of newsprint, pencil

Activity: Place a half-sheet of newspaper on a flat, smooth wall. Have the children rub the paper with a pencil held flat against the wall to create static electricity.

Observations: What happens to the paper after you've rubbed the pencil against it? What happens to the paper after a few minutes have passed?

Things to Wonder About: What makes the paper stick to the wall? Why did the paper fall after a few minutes had passed?

How can you make a light bulb shine?

Materials: #6 dry cell battery (1.5 volts), insulated copper wire, knife or scissors, 1.5 volt light bulb, 1.5 volt socket

Preparation: Strip the insulation off both ends of the wire.

Activity: Discuss the names of the materials you're using: battery, wire, light bulb, and light socket. Loosen the dry cell terminal cap, hook the end of wire beneath it, and tighten the cap. Loosen a socket screw, hook the other end of the wire around it, and tighten it. Complete the loop by hooking the other wire around the socket screw and dry cell.

Observations: What happens when the wires are all connected? What happens when you disconnect one of the wires?

Things to Wonder About: What other things use batteries? What electrical appliances use wires?

How can you light a flashlight bulb?

Materials: Size D battery, flashlight bulb, #22 or 24 bell wire

Activity: Put the bulb bottom on the raised end of the battery. Touch one wire end to the metal side of the bulb or wrap the wire end tightly around the end of the bulb. Touch the other wire end to the battery bottom.

Observations: What happens when the wire touches the bulb and the bottom of the battery? What happens when you remove one end of the wire?

Things to Wonder About: What would happen if you touched a different part of the battery with the wire?

Can you light one bulb with two batteries?

Materials: Two size D batteries, flashlight bulb, bell wire

Activity: Put the batteries end to end, with the raised end of one touching the recessed end of the other. Wrap wire around the flashlight bulb, and touch the wire to the raised end of one of the batteries. Let the other end of the wire touch the recessed end of the other battery. Then move the batteries so that their recessed ends touch, and touch the wire to both ends.

Observations: What happened when you touched the wire to the battery ends the first time? What happened after you moved the batteries?

Things to Wonder About: How is a flashlight like this? Look at a flashlight. Take it apart, and put it back together again.

Chapter Two:

Science & the Curriculum

LANGUAGE ARTS

Appliance Puzzles

Materials: Magazines or catalogs, scissors, oaktag, glue, clear adhesive paper, small boxes or plastic bags

Preparation: Cut out large pictures of electrical appliances from magazines or catalogs. Glue them on oaktag, and cover them with clear adhesive paper. Cut the pictures into puzzle pieces. Store each puzzle in a box or plastic bag.

Activity: Have the children put the puzzles together and identify the electrical appliances. Ask the children how the appliance is used. Ask them what type of energy the appliance uses and what it would be like if we didn't have this appliance.

Variation: Older children can write down their answers.

Switches On & Off

Materials: Magazines or catalogs, scissors, oaktag, glue, clear adhesive paper, three boxes, marker

Preparation: Cut out pictures of appliances and machines with switches (television, electric skillet, radio, iron, coffee maker, light switch, lamps, electric drill, computer, microwave oven). Glue the pictures on oaktag, and cover them with clear adhesive paper. Label each box with a picture indicating push, pull, or turn.

Activity: Discuss switches and how we use them. Point out any switches in the room and what they're used for. Show the children examples of switches that are pushed, pulled, and turned. Emphasize the antonyms "on" and "off," "up" and "down," "left" and "right" when discussing the switches. Have the children classify the pictures by placing them in the appropriate box. Explain that some pictures might belong in more than one box.

Variation: Older children can practice writing the words push, pull, turn, on, off, up, down, left, and right.

Magnetic Fishing

Materials: Magnet, string, ruler or stick, scissors, construction paper, markers, stapler, box or plastic tub

Preparation: Make a magnetic fishing pole by tying one end of a string to a magnet and the other end to a ruler or stick. Have the children draw and cut out fish from construction paper, drawing eyes, mouth, and fins with the markers. Staple the middle of each fish. Label the fish with uppercase or lowercase letters. (For older children, use vocabulary words.)

Activity: Create a fish pond by spreading out the fish in the box or tub. Have the children use the magnetic fishing pole to fish for letters or words. The children can name the letters as they fish them out. Have them think of a word that begins with that letter. Or have the children pull out matching uppercase and lowercase letters.

Variation: Older children can fish for vocabulary words, saying the words as they pull them out.

Mechanical or Electrical

Materials: Magazines or catalogs, scissors, oaktag, glue, clear adhesive paper, two boxes, paper, crayons or markers

Preparation: Cut out pictures of objects using mechanical or electrical energy (hand can opener, electric can opener, carpet sweeper, vacuum cleaner, egg beater, electric mixer, food grinders, food processors, manual typewriter, electric typewriter, manual pencil sharpener, electric pencil sharpener). Glue the pictures on oaktag and cover them with clear adhesive paper. Draw a hand on one of the boxes and an electrical plug on the other.

Activity: Have the children sort the pictures into those that use mechanical energy and those that use electrical energy by putting them in the appropriate boxes. Ask the children if they can think of a machine that uses both mechanical and electrical energy. Have the children draw a picture of a machine and dictate a story about it.

Variation: Older children can write down their stories about a machine.

Electric Riddles

Materials: Magazines or catalogs, scissors, oaktag, glue, clear adhesive paper

Preparation: Cut out pictures of electrical appliances, glue them on oaktag, and cover them with clear adhesive paper.

Activity: Distribute the pictures to the children. Have the children make up riddles about their pictures: for example, "I am in the kitchen, I keep food cold, and I begin with *r*. What am I?" Have the children take turns presenting their riddles for the other children to answer.

Machine Sounds

Materials: Tape, tape recorder, chart paper, marker

Preparation: Record the sounds of different machines (vacuum, doorbell, blender, car, electric saw, clock, teakettle toaster, telephone, computer keyboard, can opener, toilet).

Activity: Have the children listen to the tape and try to identify the sounds they hear. List the machines on chart paper. Ask the children to tell you where they might hear those sounds and what type of energy the machines use.

Variation: Older children can write down the machines in the order that they hear them.

MATH

Wheeling Widths

Materials: Yarn or string, scissors, chart paper, marker

Activity: Take the children outside to look at wheels on bicycles, wagons, and other things that move. Have the children identify the tires as wide or narrow. Ask them which tires they think are the widest and which are the narrowest. Then have them measure the widths with yarn or string. Inside, make a graph of tire widths. Draw a picture on chart paper of the vehicle. Next to the picture, paste the yarn or string that represents the width of its tire.

Variation: Older children can use a tape measure and record the widths of the tire wheels in inches or centimeters.

Coffee Counting

Materials: Coffee beans, clear measuring cup, coffee grinder, electric coffee machine, water

Preparation: Have the children examine the coffee beans.

Activity: Show the children a cup of coffee beans. Have the children guess how many beans are in the cup. Write down the estimates. Count the coffee beans and see whose guess was closest. Ask the children how many cups of coffee the coffee beans will make when they are ground up and put in a coffee machine. Grind the coffee beans, make coffee, and count the cups made.

Appliance Survey

Materials: Magazines or catalogs, scissors, glue, chart paper, marker

Preparation: Make a chart for the appliances that will be surveyed, using a picture to identify each appliance.

Activity: Discuss appliances and machines used in the kitchen (oven, microwave, refrigerator, coffee maker, electric can opener, food processor, electric mixer, blender, toaster oven, ice cream maker, popcorn popper). Survey parents or teachers, asking them which appliances they have. Add up the totals on the chart and compare the results.

Magnetic Shapes

Materials: Pipe cleaners magnet, scissors or knife

Activity: Have the children make geometric shapes using the pipe cleaners. Then have them pick up the shapes, using the magnet. Talk about what makes the shapes stick to the magnet. Take a pipe cleaner apart, and have the children examine the wire inside. Have the children count the number of shapes they have created.

How Many Wheels?

Materials: Toys with wheels, paper and pencil or numeral cards

Activity: Have the children look at the toys and name and discuss what they are. Have the children count the number of wheels on each toy and write the corresponding numeral or match it with a numeral card.

Variation: Older children can look at two toys and add the total number of wheels.

SOCIAL LIVING

Energy Community Helpers

Materials: Magazines and catalogs, scissors, oaktag, glue, clear adhesive paper, markers

Preparation: Cut out pictures of workers using different types of energy (firefighter, electrician, phone line worker, TV repairperson, jackhammer operator, computer operator, construction worker). Glue the pictures on oaktag, and cover them with clear adhesive paper.

Activity: Show the pictures of the community helpers. Have the children identify what each person does. Talk about the types of energy the people use or deal with in their work. Discuss the importance of the work these people do for us.

Variation: Substitute words for the pictures for older children.

Saving Energy

Materials: Chart paper, marker, pictures of energy wasting and energy saving situations

Preparation: Contact the local utilities company to get pictures of ways we waste energy and ways we can save energy. Or check the library for books or magazine articles on energy conservation.

Activity: Discuss energy conservation. Explain that energy conservation is saving our energy supplies. Ask the children what they think it would be like if one day they woke up and didn't have any energy left. Have them think of ways we waste energy and ways we can save energy. Show the pictures, and have the children discuss what is going on in each one. Make a chart of ways we waste energy and things we can do to conserve energy.

Variation: Older children can make their own charts of energy wasting and energy saving.

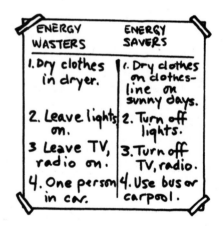

ENERGY WASTERS	ENERGY SAVERS
1. Dry clothes in dryer.	1. Dry clothes on clothes-line on sunny days.
2. Leave lights on.	2. Turn off lights.
3 Leave TV, radio on.	3. Turn off TV, radio.
4. One person in car.	4. Use bus or carpool.

Safe and Not Safe

Materials: Poster board, marker, crayons, pictures of safe and unsafe uses of electricity

Preparation: Contact the local utilities company for pictures relating to the safe use of electricity.

Activity: Discuss electrical safety practices with the children. Have the children look at the ways electricity is used in the room. Discuss the dangers of overloading outlets and of using frayed cords and broken plugs. Look at a fuse box and explain how it helps keep us safe. Show pictures of safe and unsafe electrical practices. Have the children tell you the things they've learned about using electricity safely, and make a chart. Let the kids illustrate the chart, and post it in the room where everyone can see it.

Fire Safety

Materials: Fire extinguisher, smoke alarm, rope ladder, fire stairway or exit

Activity: Discuss what to do in case of a fire. Show the children things in the room or building that are used in case of a fire. Point out fire extinguishers, smoke alarms, and fire exits. If applicable, show the children how to use a rope ladder. Discuss how a smoke alarm works and what we should do when one goes off. Go through a few practice fire drills, asking and answering questions, until the children understand exactly what they should do in case of a fire.

Chapter Three:

Science & the Creative Arts

ART

Wheel Mural

Materials: Paper towels, Styrofoam meat tray, paint, toys with wheels, brown kraft paper, pasta wheel shapes, glue

Preparation: Put paper towels in the meat tray to act as a blotter, and pour paint in the tray.

Activity: Have the children place each toy in the paint, and then make wheel tracks on the paper. Have them compare the wheel tracks that they have made. Then have the children decorate their mural by gluing pasta wheels on the paper.

Ball Painting

Materials: Paper, round cake pan, scissors, paint, spoon, small rubber balls

Preparation: Cut paper to fit the cake pan. Place the paper in the pan. Spoon a small amount of paint on the paper.

Activity: Put the rubber balls in the pan. Have the children make an inclined plane by tilting the pan back and forth. The rubber balls will roll around and create designs. Remove the paper from the pan, and let the paint dry.

Wire Sculptures

Materials: Colored wire (telephone companies will often make donations), pencil, Styrofoam pieces

Preparation: Cut the wire into strips varying from 6" to 10" in length.

Activity: Have the children bend, twist, or twirl the wire to create their sculptures. Demonstrate how to make spirals by wrapping wire around a pencil and pulling the pencil out. Then put the spirals in the Styrofoam base.

Candles

Materials: Egg carton or half-pint milk carton, candle wick (available at craft stores), scissors, candle wax or parafin, broken crayons, coffee can, pan, stove or hot plate.

Preparation: Cut and place a candle wick in each section of the egg carton or in the half-pint carton. (If using a half-pint carton, tie a pencil to the wick and rest it on top of the carton.)

Activity: Let the children decide what color they want their candles to be. Place the color crayon and some wax in the coffee can. Fill the pan halfway with water. Put the coffee can in the pan, and heat it until the wax melts. Then pour the wax into an egg-carton section or half-pint carton. Let the wax harden overnight. Then help the children remove their candles.

Campfire Collage

Materials: Lunch bags, yellow oaktag, twigs, leaves, sticks, newspapers, wood pieces and shavings, glue

Preparation: Go for a nature walk, and collect items that would be used to start a campfire. Collect the items in lunch bags.

Activity: Have the children design a campfire collage by gluing the found items on oaktag.

Magnet Collage

Materials: Red or orange oaktag, gray construction paper, pencil, scissors, glue, junk box, magnet

Preparation: Collect objects a magnet attracts (bottle caps, hair pins, paper clips, nails, pipe cleaners, twist ties, washers, soft wire) and objects a magnet repels. Cut out a pattern of a horseshoe magnet.

Activity: Have the children trace and cut out horseshoe magnets from the oaktag. Paste gray construction paper on the north and south poles of the magnet. Have the children explore the junk box, using a real magnet. Have them paste the objects the magnet attracts on the horseshoe magnet they have created.

Gadget Collage

Materials: Shoe-box lid, assorted mechanical hardware (screws, nuts, springs, washers, bottle tops, paper clips, nails), glue, silver or gold spray paint

Activity: Have the children glue the hardware on the bottom of the shoe-box lid so that it looks like a picture frame. When the glue dries, spray paint it silver or gold. This makes a nice Father's Day or Mother's Day present!

CREATIVE MOVEMENT

Blackout

Activity: Have the children pretend they're caught in a blackout, and there's no electricity. Give them examples of what it would be like: You turn on a switch, and nothing happens. You turn on the oven, and it doesn't cook your dinner. It's nighttime, and you can't see. Have the children brainstorm ways they would deal with these problems. After you've discussed their ideas, have them act out the situations. Children can pretend to be using flashlights by walking around with arms outstretched in front of their bodies, their fingers and hands flickering light. Children can impersonate candles by walking around with their arms overhead and the palms of their hands joined together. Have them sway their arms back and forth as the flames flicker and sway.

Strong Attractions

Activity: Have the children work with partners. One child pretends to be a magnet, and the other child pretends to be the object. Call out the names of different objects. If the object would stick to a magnet, the partners stick together by standing side by side or by standing back to back. For example, if you called out "nail," the partners would move together. If you called out "cotton," the partners would stay apart.

Pantomime Plugs

Materials: Pictures of electrical appliances, large paper bag

Preparation: Put the pictures of electrical appliances in a large paper bag.

Activity: Each child selects a picture from the paper bag and pantomimes it for others to guess what it is. For example, for a clothes dryer, a child could pantomime taking clothes out of a washing machine and putting them in a dryer, watching them spin around and around until they're dry. For a stereo, a child could pretend to put on a record and sing and dance. Other good appliances for this activity are hair driers, vacuums, toasters, typewriters, radios, and televisions.

Magnetic Necklaces

Materials: Paper clips, construction paper, magnets

Preparation: Distribute 20-30 paper clips on a piece of construction paper and two small magnets to each pair of children.

Activity: The children work with partners to see who can build the longest necklace chain of paper clips by attracting them with a magnet. Have the children pick up the paper clips with only their magnets, not their hands. The children hook the paper clips that they have picked up, making a paper clip necklace. After 10-15 minutes, the children can compare their necklaces to see who has the longest magnetic chain. They can then fasten the two ends of the paper-clip chain and create their own magnetic necklaces.

Variation: Form people chains. One person can pretend to be a giant magnet and the others are the paper clips. Each time the giant magnet attracts someone, he or she adds to the chain by holding hands. This continues until a people chain is formed that moves around the room in a snake-like fashion.

Steep, Steep, Slopes

Activity: Have the children pretend they're riding bicycles on a road. All of a sudden they come to a steep hill. It takes a lot of energy to peddle up that hill. They're using a lot of energy, and they're sweating. They have to peddle very hard. They peddle so hard, they get tired. Finally, they have to get off and push that bicycle up the hill. When they reach the top, they hop on the bicycle and coast down the other side. Have the children brainstorm other vehicles that they might use (skateboard, wagon).

Get Me Up There

Activity: Have the children pretend they're on the bottom level in an apartment building and they need to get to the third floor. Ask them to show you how they are going to get up to the third floor. Suggestions are walking (walking movement), stairs (climbing movement), fire escape (climbing movement), ramps (rolling around on the floor), elevator (squat up and down quickly), escalator (climbing movement).

Musical Seesaws

Materials: Music with a steady one-two beat

Activity: Have the children work in partners. Have them pretend that they are on seesaws. When one partner stands up, the other partner squats down. When the music stops, both partners should be standing — balancing the seesaw.

Fire Extinguisher Tag

Activity: Have some children pretend to be blazing, hot fires and have other children pretend to be fire extinguishers. The fire extinguishers sit down as the other children pantomime the beginning of a fire: The fire is just beginning to burn. (The children squat down close to the floor.) The flames are getting a little bigger. (The children kneel.) The wind is picking up. (The children sway back and forth on their knees.) Now the fire is blazing hot. (The children jump up and down.) The fire is spreading. (The children run around.) Here come the fire extinguishers! (The fire extinguishers catch and tag the fire children.) When a fire child has been tagged, the fire extinguisher says "Zzzzzzzzzzzap," and the fire child is extinguished and lies down. After all fire children are lying down, the fire extinguishers can also rest.

Fast, Friendly Firefighters

Activity: Talk about how a firefighter puts out a fire. Then have the children act out each part: The firefighters are asleep. (The children lie down.) The fire bell rings, "Ding! Ding! Ding!" (They get up and act out getting dressed.) They slide down the pole. (The children stoop and stand.) The firefighters get in the fire truck and drive to the fire. (They pretend to drive a truck.) They unwind the hose. (The children pretend they are pulling on a long hose.) The firefighters squirt water on the flames. (They make hissing noises and point the hose to the right, to the left, and at the ceiling.) Then they climb ladders to the second floor to rescue someone who's trapped. (The children make climbing motions.) The firefighters climb down the ladder. (They take slow steps backward.) They wind up the hose. (The children make circular motions with their arms.) Then the firefighters drive back to the fire station. (They pretend to drive a truck.)

LITERATURE

MECHANICAL ENERGY

Gibbons, Gail. *Up Goes the Skyscraper!* Macmillan, New York, 1986.

—————. *New Road.* Thomas Y. Crowell, New York, 1983.

Gordon, Sharon. *Tick Tock Clock.* Troll Associates, Mahwah, N.J., 1982.

Hoban, Tana. *Dig, Drill, Dump, Fill.* Greenwillow, New York, 1975.

Piper, Watty. *The Little Engine That Could.* Putnam, New York, 1981.

Rockwell, Ann and Harlow. *Machines.* Macmillan, New York, 1972.

—————. *Toolbox.* Macmillan, New York, 1971.

—————. *Big Wheels.* E.P. Dutton, New York, 1986.

MAGNETIC ENERGY

Ames, Gerald, and Wyler, Rose. *Prove It!* Harper & Row, New York, 1963.

Branley, Franklyn, and Vaughnan, Eleanor. *Mickey's Magnet.* Thomas Y. Crowell, New York, 1956.

Kirkpatrick, Rena K. *Look at Magnets.* Raintree Children's Press, Milwaukee, 1978.

RADIANT ENERGY

Averill, Esther. *Fire Cat.* Harper & Row, New York, 1960.

Berenstain, Stan and Jan. *The Berenstain Bears Go to Camp.* Random House, New York, 1982.

Bundt, Nancy. *Fire Station Book.* Carolrhoda Books, Minneapolis, 1981.

Gibbons, Gail, *Fire! Fire!* Harper & Row. New York, 1987.

Rockwell, Anne. *Fire Engines.* E.P. Dutton, New York, 1986.

Satchwell, John. *Fire.* Dial Books, New York, 1984.

ELECTRICAL ENERGY

Bailey, Mark W. *Electricity.* Raintree Children's Press, Milwaukee, 1978.

Bains, Rae. *Discovering Electricity.* Troll Associates, Mahwah, N.J., 1982.

Podendorf, Illa. *Energy.* Raintree Children's Press, Milwaukee, 1982.

ABOUT THE AUTHOR

Lynn Cohen received her B.S. in education from S.U.N.Y. at New Paltz and M.S. in remedial reading from Johns Hopkins University. She is currently pursuing doctoral studies in early childhood education. She teaches early childhood and elementary education at S.U.N.Y. College at Old Westbury and kindergarten for the East Williston School District in New York. She also conducts in-service workshops for early childhood teachers. She has authored three other books, *Me and My World, Exploring My World,* and *Fairy Tale World* and has contributed articles for *Pre-K Today.*